# SEVEN STAGES OF HEALING

> *"These things I have spoken unto you, that in me ye might have peace. In the world ye shall have tribulation: but be of good cheer; I have overcome the world." John 16:33 (KJV)*

Amanda Dalton

# PREFACE

Words of encouragement and hope in a devotional format. Words that will breathe life into your soul, and comfort you during one of the most difficult things we face as human beings: loss. We all go through the stages of grief in our own way. There are five main stages of grief; however, there are two that often get overlooked. I hope that this message will bless you and help you to heal.

*"These things I have spoken unto you, that in me ye might have peace. In the world ye shall have tribulation: but be of good cheer; I have overcome the world." John 16:33 (KJV)*

Everyone deals with grief in their own way. I do not pretend to know what every person will go through; however, I know one thing with certainty; God never changes. God is a God of love, and He loves his people. He knew what sin would do to the world, so He sent his only Son to die on the cross, to give us hope for a better tomorrow (John 3:16, John 10:10). There is still a thief that seeks to destroy and steal any joy or blessing we hope of having, but when Jesus died on the cross He overcame anything we might face. That's easy to say; we are the ones left on this earth going through such pain and tribulation. But, Jesus is here to help us through, I know this because He has helped me in my healing process. I have written this short book, with the hopes that it would help you through your time of difficulty. Everyone will deal with each stage differently, but most certainly these are stages of grieving that for the most part we all face. I hope that these scriptures and encouraging words will cause you to draw closer to God and allow Him to breathe life and hope back into your heart. Be blessed....

> *"The Spirit of God hath made me, and the breath of the Almighty hath given me life." Job 33:4 (KJV)*

# DENIAL

> *To everything there is a season, and a time to every purpose under heaven: A time to be born, and a time to die; a time to plant, and a time to pluck up that which is planted; a time to kill, and a time to heal; a time to break down, and a time to build up; A time to weep, and a time to laugh; a time to mourn, and a time to dance. –*
> *Ecclesiastes 3:1-4 (KJV)*

It is always a shock when we lose someone we hold dear. Whether we plan for it, or it happens suddenly, it's never an easy thing to accept. Our bodies have natural defenses that will try to block pain when something tries to cause us physical harm.

The loss of a loved one causes every part of our body, mind, and spirit to become numb. When I lost my mother in 2011 tragically, I refused to believe she was gone. I could not comprehend how that was possible. A friend I had seen one morning in church, an hour later was on life support due to a car accident. How could this be? When I just saw this person very much alive, it doesn't make sense. Where are they?

The bible says that there is a time and a season for every purpose under heaven. We are all built with a purpose for this life, but it is just a part of it. Though we must face death at some point, it is not the end. Jesus died on the cross so that we might gain eternal life

(John 3:16), regardless of the sinful world we find ourselves in. The sickness, disease, heartaches and sorrows we face on this earth will all be wiped away. Not that we cannot find joy and blessing in the life we lead, but there is so much more waiting for us in eternity.

*"And God shall wipe away all tears from their eyes; and there shall be no more death, neither sorrow, nor crying, neither shall there be any more pain: for the former things are passed away."* Revelation 21:4 (KJV)

# ANGER

> *"Be ye angry, and sin not: let not the sun go down upon your wrath." Ephesians 4:6 (KJV)*

It is the easiest thing in the world to act out in anger when something horrible comes against us. We seek to find and place blame, to make sense of what's happening. Jesus warns us not to sin in our time of anger. It is natural to feel anger, yet we should not act out in anger. Instead we should find a prayer closet and talk to God, talk to someone you trust, and learn to rely on our brothers and sisters in the body of Christ to lend an ear; to help us work through our emotions, that's what it was created for. (1 Corinthians 12:26)

We do not want to damage relationships with those around us, or foolishly charge God in our time of hardship. It only creates further wounds in our own hearts and those around us. If you cannot control your emotions, take a moment, quiet the negative talk by asking God to take captive your thoughts, and then approach with a clear head.

*We demolish arguments and every pretension that sets itself up against the knowledge of God, and we take captive every thought to make it obedient to Christ. 2 Corinthians 10:5*

When my mother died, I was angry with God. I was angry at my own father and inwardly I blamed him, even though it wasn't his fault. We all make our own choices, no one forces us to do things. I wanted to blame God because I had prayed so many times for her deliverance from alcohol and salvation. Unfortunately, the person that doesn't accept the help cannot be helped. It was not God's fault, or my fathers. I humbly came back to earth after being told by my pastor that I need not foolishly charge God. Do I believe she is with Jesus? I don't know. But I don't dwell on that, because God is a just God. (Psalm 25:8)

He has bottled up every tear and every prayer, and has answered and attended to everyone, even if we are not fully aware of it. One day He will wipe every tear. If you find yourself crying out to God over any circumstance, you will find peace in His comfort. A supernatural peace that passes all understanding. (Philippians 4:7)

Sometimes it hits me, and I feel sorrow, that's natural, but I know the God I serve is a God of love. He can do anything, even in the last few moments of a person's life. He is not limited by time or space, and He is faithful to those who call upon His name. We may not understand everything, but one day we will. Could God have saved her? Yes. But, He didn't. There is a purpose in everything, even pain.

We all have choices to make in life, and we must live with the consequences of those choices, and I did all I could through prayer and just loving them like Jesus would. I do also believe that God forgives us in our anger, He understands more than anyone the emotions we go through in this life. Jesus himself experienced every emotion that we might ever face and took them to the cross of Calvary. He took out the garbage and the ashes, so that we could find beauty once again (Isaiah 61:3) in the life God intended for us to live; in union with Him. (John 10:10)

*"For we do not have a high priest who is unable to empathize with our weaknesses, but we have one who has been tempted in every way, just as we are—yet he did not sin." Hebrews 4:15 (KJV)*

*"In all this Job sinned not, nor charged God foolishly." Job 1:22 (KJV)*

# BARGAINING

> *"Saying, Father, if thou be willing, remove this cup from me: nevertheless not my will, but thine, be done." Luke 22:42 (KJV)*

Jesus himself bargained with God. Before He was about to give up his spirit on the cross; being filled with all the sin of the world, in a moment of weakness and delirium, cried out to God. When we are at our worst, it is natural to cry out for the impossible. It was not impossible for God to take the pain away from Jesus; but God knew that once His will was fulfilled, something beautiful followed – the bridge between God and man would be restored. The dispensation of Grace could now come to fruition. Jesus would reign on the throne, and we can now reign with Him forever if we accept His offer of grace.

Life is not always easy, but Jesus is very much alive and active; knowing everything we face, as He had experienced it in the flesh. Whenever I am scared to lose someone I love, of course I bargain with God to save them. But I have learned that God's will must also come to pass regardless of how I feel, so I also pray for Gods will.

There is a time and a season for everything to come to pass. (Ecclesiastes 3:1)

God knows the beginning from the end. Although not everything that happens in this world is how God intended – due to sin; God can work everything for the greater good (Romans 8:28). It is OKAY to cry out to God and be HONEST, God loves an honest heart. He knows our hearts greatest desire, and our every thought before we even think it. Just know that God will help us through our time of doubt and unbelief, and that this world is only a small stopping point on our journey to eternity.

Death is not the end, though it may be hard, it is just a reminder that the time is coming near when Jesus will come back, and we will be reunited with those we love. The sadness will not stay forever (Psalm 30:5). The Lord sticks close to the broken hearted and helps them heal. (Psalm 34:18) You will never forget your loved ones, but you will learn to move on with life in remembrance of them, and the hope that Jesus gives us for eternity (1 John 2:25).

*"I am Alpha and Omega, the beginning and the ending, saith the Lord, which is, and which was, and which is to come, the Almighty." Revelation 1:8 (KJV)*

# DEPRESSION

> *"Blessed are they that mourn: for they shall be comforted."* Matthew 5:4 (KJV)

There comes a time, just after you feel you have made progress, that a deep sadness will overcome you. This is a very crucial time to be honest with yourself and let yourself mourn. Cry out to God, He is always there to comfort you in your time of need. People may try very hard to encourage you, yet nothing will seem to truly help. It will for a moment, but it is when you find yourself alone that depression tries to creep in and steal all joy from you.

This can be a very crucial time as some people deal with this face on in a healthy way, and others might turn to ineffective coping mechanisms such as ignorance, alcohol or drugs. Trying to numb the pain is never the way to cope. You need to accept your feelings to deal with them. It can be hard to work through, but once you do, you will find freedom in it.

You may start to think about things you wish you had done or said. But this is not the time to look back in regret. This is a time to cherish the good memories and move forward. Our loved ones wouldn't have it any other way. We are a selfish people in a sense, we want to keep our loved ones here for US, but imagine all the wonderful things that lie ahead of them. There's a song that says, "You wouldn't give up the streets of Gold, now that you know."

If there were things left unsaid or undone (and there always will be for everyone) simply forgive yourself. Your loved one certainly would not want you to live in such a depressed state. They would want you to move on with your life, for them. And that just means you will have more to talk about in eternity! Although I doubt any of those concerns will ever be remembered.

Sometimes it helps to speak out loud, when you are going through times of reflection. Speak out loud as if you are talking to your loved one, say what you need to say, even if it seems silly. After my mother died, there was so much I wish I had of said to her, more I wish I could have done. I know it is unrealistic, since our loved ones are passed on, but at the same time, speaking my thoughts out loud helped me gain that absolution I needed. A deep relief followed … I prayed that God would relay the message to her for me. I felt a sense of peace come over me in that moment, that allowed me to move forward in the healing process.

Sometimes our loved ones might leave us with things that were unresolved. Perhaps you feel angry at this person for something they did or said, and you feel bad about it because they have passed away. This is where forgiveness comes in. Forgiving your loved one and letting them go is the absolute key for your own personal healing. You also need to learn to forgive yourself; we are imperfect beings. Even if it is something unjustifiable. Forgiveness does not justify, it sets you free. God is the judge, not us. Holding onto bitterness can do a lot of damage over time.

*"Forbearing one another, and forgiving one another, if any man has a quarrel against any: even as Christ forgave you, so also do ye."* Colossians 3:13(KJV)

*"Casting all your care upon him; for he careth for you."* 1 Peter 5:7 (KJV)

# ACCEPTANCE

> *"For as the heavens are higher than the earth, so are my ways higher than your ways, and my thoughts than your thoughts." Isaiah 55:9 (KJV)*

There comes a time toward the end of the grieving process, that you begin to accept things for what they are. You won't have overcome everything you will face; however, you will have a better grasp on how to move forward. This isn't to say that you will not have times where you regress to some of the sad emotions you were experiencing, but you will be better equipped on how to deal with them when they come.

God's thoughts are higher than our thoughts. We cannot always wrap our brain around everything in this life, but we can hold onto the assurance that Jesus holds our every moment. He knows what each day will bring and prepares to carry us through it. We simply need to hold his hand and keep in constant prayer.

Even for those who don't necessarily believe in God, everyone prays. Prayer is powerful, and has the power to heal, mend a broken heart, set you free. Simply call on the name of Jesus if you don't know what to say, He will meet you where you are. When your heart breaks, so does God's. (John 11:35) Jesus wept when Lazarus died, even though He knew He was about to perform a miracle, and bring Him back to life, He felt the hurt of what had happened to Lazarus. And the pain his family was feeling at that moment.

> "And the LORD, he it is that doth go before thee; he will be with thee, he will not fail thee, neither forsake thee: fear not, neither be dismayed." Deuteronomy 31:8 (KJV)

> "Rejoicing in hope; patient in tribulation; continuing instant in prayer." Romans 12:12 (KJV)

There are many things we will face in this life, the waters are not always calm; we go through storm after storm in this life, but Jesus is always there to bring us safely to shore, just take a step of faith(Matthew 14:22-33) Aren't you glad your lifeguard walks on water? There is no situation impossible for God to help you through. You simply need to ask him to come into your heart and help to heal it.

> "For with God nothing shall be impossible." Luke 1:37 (KJV)

> When thou passest through the waters, I will be with thee; and through the rivers, they shall not overflow thee: when thou walkest through the fire, thou shalt not be burned; neither shall the flame kindle upon thee. Isaiah 43:2 (KJV)

# HOPE

> *" For I know the plans I have for you," declares the Lord, "plans to prosper you and not to harm you, plans to give you hope and a future." Jeremiah 29:11 (NIV)*

These last two stages are not listed as the main five stages of grief. One can forget that after you have come through tribulation, there is a light at the end. Once weeping has endured, it is meant to be followed with Joy. (Psalm 30:5)

This stage is one of Hope and one of Victory. The mind, and our emotions can be the hardest thing to overcome. I guess we would never know victory without a battle, or peace without absence of it.

God has a great plan and purpose for our lives, and He equips us for success in His word. The most important thing we must remember at this stage, is that the body of Christ is our life support. When one part of the body hurts, we need the other parts of the body to keep it going. Like red blood cells rushing to the site of an injury, the body of Christ is there to support the healing process.

We think of life support as some machinery that we are hooked up to, that helps us keep breathing. I can say with certainly, that once you have overcome an obstacle in life, the enemy will try to come back and steal your joy once again, so we need support through those times. The enemy has no power, other than what we allow him. There is a spiritual thief in the world that seeks to destroy, but we have a Heavenly Father that seeks to give life.

> *"So we, being many, are one body in Christ, and every one members one of another."* Romans 12:5 (KJV)

> *"The thief comes only to steal and kill and destroy; I have come that they may have life, and have it to the full."* John 10:10 (NIV)

God didn't plan for us to "just get by" He planned for us to live life to the fullest. This is nothing compared to eternity, but we can live as a blessed people now. Now is the time to find your purpose and live it! Without a vision, we as a people perish. We always need a goal to work toward. Even if you start small, make small reachable goals for every day, week, month, year. Whatever it takes to keep moving. It is all too easy to be overcome by our sorrows, and begin to die spiritually, which affects our physical health as well. It is good to grieve the people we love, it means that we had something extremely valuable in our lives, but we also must keep living *our* lives while we are still here.

# NEW LIFE

> "Behold, I will do a new thing; now it shall spring forth; shall ye not know it? I will even make a way in the wilderness, and rivers in the desert." Isaiah 43:19 (KJV)

Whenever one door closes, another always opens. (Revelation 3:7) This is also a famous quote of Alexander Graham Bell. This saying does not mean that God is always going to open another door immediately; however, I've come to learn that when God shuts one door, He will open another, and usually a better one. One that no man can alter.

When one journey ends, or one part of your life ends, there is always something waiting to be birthed in us. God is always looking to take everything that we go through, and use it to grow us, and make us into the men and women we were designed to be.

Every person that impacts our life, we take a small piece of them with us. I know that as I learn and grow, I consistently am reminded of things my own personal role models and mentors have passed on to me. Even if they are not here any longer, we have a responsibility with the gifts we have been given, to not sit idle, but use it wisely. To carry on the work laid out before us, for the next generation. If we have breath, we still have a purpose and a future to fulfill.

Maybe you have had people in your life that have hurt you, or you are still struggling with grief today over someone or something even. Now is the time to face those emotions head on, ask God to break the chains over your life, and live a life of freedom and liberty in Christ.

The previous devotional talked of making goals. God absolutely intends for us to have dreams and goals. He gives us dreams for a reason, so dream big! Pray God's will in your life, and you will never falter. Make your loved ones proud.

> *"Commit to the Lord whatever you do, and he will establish your plans." Proverbs 16:3 (NIV)*

If you aren't sure what you are meant to do going forward, ask God to reveal it to you. He is excited to help you get back on track and find new hope and joy in our purposes going forward. Jesus died so we could do exactly that.

We are not meant to live in the past but to move forward with strength from our journey, and the things we have overcome. We are more than conquerors through Him who loved us. (Romans 8:37) The saying "what doesn't kill us makes us stronger" I believe to be true. We become wiser with every obstacle we face. God knows what we can bear, and for the things we can't, He is right there beside us, carrying us or walking before us.

The Israelites came through many trials before reaching their promised destination; for forty years, they wandered. (Joshua 5:6).

You may feel as though you are in a desert place now, but do not give up hope, the rain will come, and He will make a way where there seems to be no way (Isaiah 43:16-19). The comforter will come to sustain you, dry and collect every tear drop, and supply all your needs in Christ Jesus, so that you may move forward in victory. (John 14:16) Even the rose finds a way to bloom in the desert place. (Isaiah 35:1)

*You keep track of all my sorrows. You have collected all my tears in your bottle. You have recorded each one in your book. Psalm 56:8 (NLT)*

*Behold, I will do a new thing; now it shall spring forth; shall ye not know it? I will even make a way in the wilderness, and rivers in the desert. Isaiah 43:19 (KJV)*

*They did not thirst when He led them through the deserts He made the water flow out of the rock for them; He split the rock and the water gushed forth. Isaiah 48:21*

God never gave up on the Israelites no matter how much they complained, and He will never give up on us, that is a promise. (Deuteronomy 31:6) So move forward into the blessings that are in store for your life!

> *"Every ending is a new beginning. Through the grace of God, we can always start again." - Marianne Williamson*

# FOOTPRINTS IN THE SAND

One night I had a dream...

I dreamed I was walking along the beach with the Lord,
and across the sky flashed scenes from my life.
For each scene I noticed two sets of footprints in the sand;
One belonged to me, and the other to the Lord.

When the last scene of my life flashed before us,
I looked back at the footprints in the sand.
I noticed that many times along the path of my life,
there was only one set of footprints.

I also noticed that it happened at the very lowest
and saddest times in my life.
This really bothered me, and I questioned the Lord about it.
"Lord, you said that once I decided to follow you, you would walk
with me all the way.

But I have noticed that during the most troublesome times in my
life,
There is only one set of footprints.
I don't understand why in times when I needed you the most,
you should leave me.

The Lord replied, "My precious, precious
child. I love you, and I would never,
never leave you during your times of
trial and suffering.
When you saw only one set of footprints,
It was then that I carried you.

> *For I know the plans I have for you, "declares the Lord,
> "plans to prosper you and not to harm you, plans to give
> you hope and a future." Jeremiah 29:11 (NIV)*

# THIS SHIP

*This ship does journey the mighty seas.*
*By Faith these sail's will ever rise.*
*Tattered and worn, yet anchored in thee;*
*by Grace 'til the sea marry the sky.*

*Transparent to the crashing waves nigh;*
*Homeward bound for the Son hath lit the way.*
*Praises we do sing unto the blue bowled skies;*
*'til the wretched night turns to solemn day.*

*A Lighthouse in the distance, nearer and nearer still,*
*its rays soar brightly cross the skies.*
*The storm and the tempest sweep o'er the mill;*
*Pray not by strength or might but by your will.*

*This ship it Graces the dancing waves;*
*Crashing in flight; seasons pass by.*
*Rising and Kneeling they seemingly praise,*
*the creator of the birds in the sky.*

*The seas they calm at the command of the wind.*
*The glowing embers of the horizon nearer more.*
*The season has come to pass, oh mighty oars;*
*I bid you no more, oh glorious shore.*

*Captain of the vessel rises to say,*
*"Well done, thou good and faithful servant, to this day;*
*Thou has been faithful all the while,*
*I now give thee rule o'er many things."*

*May all ye weary and laden receive rest.*
*Enter thou into the joy of the Lord.*
*The time has come, to reap your reward.*
*I bid you no more, oh Glorious Shore.*

*I bid you no more.*

*© Amanda Batten 2009*

> *His lord said unto him, Well done, thou good and faithful servant: thou hast been faithful over a few things, I will make thee ruler over many things: enter thou into the joy of thy lord. Matthew 25:21 (KJV)*

Made in United States
Troutdale, OR
12/18/2024

26856617R00015